Making

THE OFFICIAL Whoopie Pie Book

Whoopies

By Nancy Griffin

Down East

Copyright © 2010 by Nancy Griffin
Front cover photograph by Mark Fleming.
Cover whoopie pie created by Amy Bouchard, Isamax Snacks Bakery.
ISBN: 978-0-89272-810-7
Library of Congress Control Number 2010920625
Printed in China
10 9 8 7

BOOKS·MAGAZINE·ONLINE
w w w . d o w n e a s t . c o m

Distributed to the trade by National Book Network

For Matthew and Meara, who
always make me want to holler,

"Whoopie!"

ISAMAX SNACKS BAKERY

3

Recipe Index

Contents

Introduction

"A book about whoopie pies?" I hear you ask. "Is there really that much to say about whoopie pies? The answer is a whopping yes!

The moment of the whoopie pie is now. These sweet treats are the ultimate comfort food. They're unpretentious and home-grown, nothing like highbrow crêpes and soufflés. Even the name is cheerful and uplifting. The definitions for *whoopie* (or *whoopee*) include "an exclamation of joy or excitement." Making whoopie means to "engage in a noisy, boisterous celebration." These definitions all aptly describe the human interaction with the whoopie pie: eating a fistful of whoopie pie in all its squishy, creamy sweetness is certainly joyful, can be exciting, and is absolutely celebratory.

Of course, the phrase "making whoopie" is also a euphemism used by the entertainment industry in the early days to suggest amorous activity while circumventing the censors. Some whoopie pie aficionados may in fact equate eating whoopies with its more salacious connotation.

This book will tell you everything you want to know about the wonderful whoopie, from its debated origins to its modern-day adaptations. And the more than a dozen recipes will have you making some whoopies (the edible kind) of your own. Happy reading, baking, and, most important, eating!

A whoopie pie's a wondrous thing,
Like newborn pups or early spring.
It fills the mouth with rapture sweet,
This yummy chocolate sandwich treat.

—Anonymous

What's a Whoopie Pie?

The whoopie pie is a nearly perfect food, if you ignore pesky little details such as calories or cholesterol. For those who love sweets, especially dark, devil's food chocolate cake and lush, creamy vanilla filling, the whoopie pie is the ultimate dessert.

It's certainly not a pie, by any stretch of the imagination. But then, neither is a Boston cream pie.

A traditional whoopie pie consists of two soft, mounded, dark chocolate cakes, each resembling the top of a well-rounded chocolate hamburger bun, generously filled with creamy white filling. Sometimes the filling layer is nearly as thick as the cake around it, making for a gooey eating experience that leaves fingers, faces, and everything within reach streaked or coated with white stuff. And that's half the fun.

There ends any agreement about what constitutes a real whoopie pie. Aficionados, however, argue over which ingredients were found in the "original" filling. Believe it or not, these treats have incited lots of discussion and passion in recent years as whoopie pie fame spreads across the country.

Even the name is not consistent, although it is not cause for dispute. In parts of Pennsylvania—residents say primarily in the central part of the state—whoopie pies

WHOOPIE
WISDOM

There are those who say the whoopie pie is the same as a moon pie, a popular snack from the southern United States, but the two are distinctly different. Moon pies are flat, hard cookies filled with marshmallow, then the entire thing's dipped in chocolate. They, too, have a long history and a few fanciful tales about their origins, but we're not going to tell them.

JEFF SCHER

are called gobs. (It's clear why *whoopie pie*, and not that other name, is sweeping the country.)

Once upon a time, hardly anyone outside New England, parts of Pennsylvania, and relocated Amish communities in other states had ever heard of a whoopie pie, but now these delectables can be found as far away as California, Texas, and Michigan. Upscale Manhattan bakeries make them. A recipe even turned up on a food blog originating in Newfoundland, Canada. Celebrity chefs sing their praises. They have been featured in national publications, high-profile TV shows, and they're on food sites all over the Web.

They've arrived.

What Really Makes It a Whoopie?

① The Way It Is Eaten: By hand, so enjoy the confection while walking, driving, golfing, or mowing the lawn.

② When It Is Eaten: Usually quite fast, but you can pop it in the freezer. The average whoopie will survive freezing unharmed.

③ How Much Is Eaten: Whoopies come in all sizes, but the hand-held, one-serving whoopie is usually around four inches in diameter.

④ What Frosting Is Eaten: One school of traditionalists insists that the original filling contains vegetable shortening. Another argues that the original filling includes marshmallow crème or Fluff.

⑤ What Flavor Is Eaten: Purists refuse to recognize many of the non-chocolate variants as whoopie pies at all. (We're not that strict!)

HERSHEY FARMS RESTAURANT AND INN

WHOOPIE
WISDOM

A WHOOPIE
IS NOT
A COOKIE

The cake parts of the whoopie
pie are sometimes called
soft cookies, but they're
usually really soft and not
really very cookielike at all.

Whoopie Wrap-Up

There used to be a traditional whoopie pie, which is
not a pie at all, but is round and made of chocolate
cake with white filling (and an everlasting debate over
the "real" filling ingredients) that originated in one
of three places (more on that next) at some unknown
time, possibly around the 1920s but maybe later, and
it might be called a gob. Nowadays there exists a dizzy-
ing array of cake and filling flavors, and the occasional
whoopie pie is not even round.

Whence Whoopies?

For many, the "true" history of the whoopie pie is about pride in the product—Mainers, Pennsylvanians, and Bostonians all claim the fame of having invented the beloved whoopie. And while people in all of those locations have theories and hold strong beliefs, so far no one has shown incontrovertible proof of the whoopie pie's origin.

Pennsylvania Whoopies & Gobs

Pennsylvania's story about the mystery-cloaked origin of the whoopie claims Amish women invented the black-and-white dessert, and the confection got its name when they packed the desserts for their children's school lunches.

If the children opened their lunch boxes and found the chocolate treat, they would invariably exclaim, "Whoopie!" The other version of the story puts the treats in the Amish husbands' lunch pails. Somehow it seems less likely that grown Amish farmers would be caught yelling "Whoopie!" at their lunch pails, but you never know.

Whether the whoopie was invented in the Keystone State or not, and even though some parts of the state still refer to it by the inglorious soubriquet of gob, Pennsylvania certainly is a hotbed of whoopie pie culture, with whoopies available at roadside stands, restaurants, bakeries, and many other venues. Pennsylvania's

The song "Makin' Whoopee" was written by Gus Kahn for a 1928 Broadway musical called *Whoopee!*, which was filmed and released in 1930 as a Hollywood movie.

annual Whoopie Pie Festival, started in 2005, was the first in the nation.

Pennsylvania is one of only two states where every resident knows what a whoopie pie is and most will tell you their grandmother made them.

The Maine Claim

The other state is Maine, where knowledgeable residents insist the pie was actually invented. The creation of the first whoopie, according to Maine legend, occurred when a woman working in a Bangor commercial bakery ended up with extra batter after making a batch of cakes. Rather than waste it, she scooped spoonfuls of the batter onto a baking tray and popped them into the oven. After they were done, she stuck the resulting mounds together with leftover frosting, and, *voilà*!

Both the Pennsylvania lunchbox moms and frugal Bangor baker stories may be apocryphal, but Maine's venerable Labadie's Bakery, established in 1917, advertises that it has been making Whoopie Pies Since 1925. Since a fire destroyed all the plant's records in the late 1960s, current owner Fabian Labadie says he can't prove it, however. These days, the Lewiston company runs twenty-four hours a day, five days a week, producing baked goods—including and especially whoopie pies—under its own name and for other private labels.

JEFF SCHER

Born in Beantown?

Boston is different. Boston has two stories, but one is surely not true because the people credited in that story flatly deny it. The other tale is easy to believe, but is not exactly proven. And for some strange reason, even though whoopie pies certainly existed in Boston since the early twentieth century, not all Boston residents remember growing up with them. But some do.

One story credits Durkee-Mower, Inc., with inventing the whoopie pie to increase sales of its product, the sticky, sweet Marshmallow Fluff that comprises half of Durkee's trademarked Fluffernutter sandwich and a bit of the filling in some whoopie pie recipes. Part of this story is true—Durkee-Mower did publish a cookbook in 1930 filled with recipes that called for Marshmallow Fluff as an ingredient. However, the claim that the *first* whoopie pie recipe appeared in the Durkee *Yummy Book* is just plain wrong.

John Durkee, fourth generation of the family that has owned Marshmallow Fluff since 1920, says the recipe did appear in the *Yummy Book*, but not until the 1970s (see recipe on page 24). The original *Yummy Book* published some forty years earlier contained no references to whoopie pies.

> Does anyone argue over the origin of the whoopee cushion? It was invented in Toronto, Canada, by rubber workers around 1930, about the same time as the whoopie pie.

The other Boston story centers on the Berwick Cake Company in Dudley Square, Roxbury. Some old-timers in Boston have told reporters they remember eating Berwick's whoopie pies growing up. The bakery itself is making no claim to have invented whoopie pies, because it went out of business in 1977. However, the name of the bakery, painted long ago on the side of the Berwick building, still remains, and current tenants in the building swear there once was another painted sign on the bricks that read "Whoopee! Pies."

Dessert Debate

Nancy Baggett, author of *The All-American Dessert Book* and *The All-American Cookie Book,* tentatively credits the Berwick Cake Company as the originator of the whoopie pie since she found no reference to whoopie pies in any Pennsylvania cookbook prior to the 1960s.

New Hampshire dietitian Peter Schlichting has researched the whoopie pie's beginnings and says the recipe appears during the Depression in recipe collections from several different states. He credits New England, particularly the Berwick folks, with creating the first whoopie pie, because a retired employee told him the company started baking them in 1926.

Alas the mystery remains unsolved.

The 5¢ Cake

Berwick Cake Company's whoopie pies were certainly in distribution throughout New England and elsewhere by 1931, because in that year an ad in New York's *Syracuse Herald* read: "Distributors for Berwick Whoopee Pie, the largest-selling 5¢ cake…" If it was "largest-selling" by June 6, 1931, it had probably been around for a while.

A Thrill in Every Bite

A 1932 ad from the Pennsylvania's *Bedford Gazette* touted a new treat: "We are now baking the latest in good things to eat—the new delicious Whoopee Pie, a chocolate cake sandwich with a tasty buttercream filling, a combination that will please the most fastidious taste. You may sample the new Whoopee Pie at either of our stores tomorrow, Saturday, April 30. There's a thrill in every bite."

WHOOPIE WISDOM

WHOOPIE WANNABEES

Drake's bakery had its Devil Dog, a dark, dry chocolate cake with a white filling, but shaped like a hot dog. Suzy Qs, a snack produced by the Hostess Cakes brand, came on the market in 1961, and although somewhat similar to whoopie pies, Suzy Qs are oblong. Much more recently, the Nabisco company introduced the Cakester, a soft sandwich closely resembling a whoopie pie, in several sizes.

*Makin' Whoopies

If there's controversy about who made whoopie pies first or what constitutes the "real" traditional ingredients, there's no serious disagreement about how to put the confections together. About the only areas where home bakers diverge is whether they drop the dollops of batter on the baking sheet with an ice cream scoop or a spoon and whether they grease the baking tray, leave it ungreased, or line it with a silicone mat or baking parchment.

A big electric mixer is a useful tool since the batter is relatively dense—it must stand up on its own without spreading all over the baking sheet and running into the other nascent whoopies. A big mixer also means you won't tire out quickly and you'll have the stamina to make many more batches of whoopies right away.

JEFF SCHER

TODAY:
WHOOPIE
PIES
✓ SUGAR ✓ COCOA
✓ EGG   ✓ VANILLA
✓ FLOUR ✓ LOVE
✓ MILK

KING ARTHUR FLOUR CO.

JEFF SCHER

WHOOPIE WISDOM

DRY OR MOIST?

One school of thought says the cakes should be relatively dry because the filling provides the moisture in a whoopie pie, and many of the whoopies sold commercially do lean more toward the dry side. In general, though, the all-natural or upscale whoopie pies tend to be moister.

But power tools are not required; a baker determined to make whoopies may do so using just a whisk, a wooden spoon, a bowl, and an oven. Never underestimate what a determined consumer or baker will go through in order to rendezvous with a whoopie. Sometimes, due to weather (or the vagaries of ingredients), the dollops of batter spread more than you would like. If you feel it's necessary to impress the folks with the perfect convexity of your whoopies, freeze the flat ones for later, or fill them and eat them all yourself when no one is looking. So long as you wash your hands and wipe your mouth afterward, no one will ever know. This stratagem provides the added benefit of allowing you to appear virtuous later, when you back away from whoopie indulgence while others are stuffing themselves.

So throw on your apron and awaken your whoopie appetite. Here are the general steps to whoopie making plus more than a half dozen classic recipes to taste-test.

KING ARTHUR FLOUR CO.

WHOOPIE WISDOM

WEB WHOOPIES

The King Arthur Flour Web site **www.kingarthurflour.com** provides recipes as well as excellent photographs that illustrate each step in the process. Any whoopie-baking neophyte with further questions about construction will find them answered there.

Onward, Whoopie Maker

Here are the steps involved in making whoopies, followed by nine of the best classic recipes out there. Some use vegetable shortening and raw egg white filling, while others include Marshmallow Fluff. Try them all, and then you and your neighbors can choose a favorite filling, buck up sides, and fight it out just like the rest of the whoopie world.

■ Find a recipe that interests you.

■ Assemble the ingredients so eggs and butter (or whatever) will be at room temperature.

■ Preheat the oven.

■ Follow recipe directions, which, for the cake, will probably include a first step of creaming the shortening and sugar, then adding eggs. When mixing liquid and dry ingredients into the batter, begin and end with dry ingredients.

■ Make sure the batter comes out fairly stiff because a runny or too-soft batter won't work. The cakes can't spread too much or they'll run into each other and won't rise up properly to be high and rounded. (*Note:* Some people complain that big whoopie pies are too high in the middle to get their mouths around. But what do they know? Don't shrink your whoopies—better to do some exercises to stretch your mouth.)

■ Scoop the batter onto a baking sheet that's either ungreased or greased, depending on the recipe, or covered with parchment paper or a silicone mat. Recipes often indicate options. Some bakers use cookie scoops, muffin scoops, or ice cream scoops (all pretty similar) for convenience and consistent size.

■ To make minis, bakers suggest using a teaspoonful, mounded, or a table-spoonful, not mounded. Minis may be made in any size you want, but watch the baking time—tiny ones won't take long.

■ Bake for the prescribed time, watching the cakes so they don't burn on the edges. (And remember: ovens may vary.)

■ Cool the baked cakes on the baking sheet briefly, then transfer them to a cooling rack. Just be sure they don't stick to the sheet.

■ Mix the filling according to the recipe, but don't apply it to the cakes until they're completely cooled.

■ Some cooks use a scoop for measuring out the filling as well. Others just use a cake frosting spreader, a knife, or a big spoon—whatever works. Spread the filling on one cake. (If you want the true whoopie pie experience, start with plenty of filling, then add more.) Place a second cake on top.

WHOOPIE WISDOM

KEEPING THEM AT THEIR PEAK

Unless they're being served right away, wrap the whoopies indi-vidually in plastic. They will grow more moist while incarcerated! And some recipes call for refrig-erating the assembled whoopie pies—especially those containing raw egg whites in the filling.

Classic Chocolate Whoopie Pies I

Here is a good old-fashioned whoopie adapted from a King Arthur Flour Company recipe. The optional espresso powder—often used in "devil's food" recipes—makes a tasty variation. If you've never had a whoopie pie, start here.

Yield: 8 large whoopie pies (about 4" diameter)

Cakes

½ cup butter

1 cup brown sugar, packed

1 teaspoon espresso powder, optional

1 teaspoon baking powder

½ teaspoon baking soda

¾ teaspoon salt

1 teaspoon vanilla extract

1 large egg

½ cup Dutch-processed cocoa

2⅓ cups King Arthur Unbleached All-Purpose Flour

1 cup milk

Filling

1 cup vegetable shortening

1 cup confectioners' sugar or glazing sugar

1⅓ cups Marshmallow Fluff or marshmallow crème

¼ teaspoon salt dissolved in 1 tablespoon water

1½ teaspoons vanilla extract

To make 16 smaller whoopie pies (about 2¾" diameter, 2½ ounces each): drop the batter onto the baking sheets in 30-gram balls, about the size of a Ping-Pong ball, or about 1¼". Bake for 11 to 12 minutes, until set. Finish as directed in the recipe.

Marshmallow Fluff is a trademarked New England product available in certain other parts of the country. Marshmallow crème, more widely available, has a thinner consistency. If you use marshmallow crème, you may need to add a bit more sugar to stiffen it up sufficiently.

JEFF SCHER

■ Preheat the oven to 350°F. Lightly grease (or line with parchment) two baking sheets.

■ In a large mixing bowl, beat together the butter, sugar, espresso powder, baking powder, baking soda, salt, and vanilla until smooth. Add the egg, again beating until smooth. Add the cocoa, stirring to combine.

■ Add the flour to the batter alternately with the milk, beating until smooth. Scrape down the sides and bottom of the bowl, and beat again briefly to soften and combine any chunky scrapings.

■ Drop the batter by the quarter-cupful onto the prepared baking sheets, leaving plenty of room between the cakes; they'll spread. A muffin scoop (a ¼ cup scoop available from bakery suppliers) works well here.

■ Bake the cakes for 15 to 16 minutes, until they're set and firm to the touch. Remove them from the oven, and cool on the sheets. While still lukewarm, use a spatula to separate them from the pan or parchment; then allow to cool completely.

■ Make the filling by beating together the shortening, sugar, and marshmallow until well combined. Dissolve the salt in the water and add to the marshmallow mixture. Add the vanilla and beat until smooth.

■ Spread the filling on the flat side of half of the cooled the cakes. Top with the remaining cakes, flat side toward the filling. Wrap individually in plastic until ready to serve.

Classic Chocolate Whoopie Pies II

A slightly different recipe from the previous one, this concoction, from the Durkee-Mower *Yummy Book*, is still a classic whoopie.

Yield: 15 whoopie pies

JEFF SCHER

Cakes

1 egg

⅓ cup vegetable oil

1 cup sugar

2 cups unsifted all-purpose flour

⅓ cup unsweetened cocoa

1 teaspoon baking soda

¼ teaspoon salt

¾ cup milk

1 teaspoon vanilla

Filling

½ cup butter or margarine

1 cup confectioners' sugar

1 cup Marshmallow Fluff (about half of a 7½-ounce jar)

1 teaspoon vanilla

■ Preheat the oven to 350°F. Grease two large cookie sheets and set aside.

■ In a large bowl, with a mixer at medium speed, beat together the egg and vegetable oil. Gradually beat in the sugar and continue beating until pale yellow in color.

■ In another bowl, combine the flour, cocoa, baking soda, and salt. In a measuring cup combine the milk and vanilla. Add flour and milk mixtures alternately to eggs and sugar, beginning and ending with the dry ingredients.

■ Drop the batter by tablespoons onto cookie sheets. These will spread a lot, so arrange only 6 cakes per sheet. Bake for about 5 minutes or until the tops spring back when lightly touched with a finger. Remove the tops to wire racks to cool.

■ In a medium bowl, with a mixer at medium speed, beat together the butter, sugar, Marshmallow Fluff, and vanilla until light and fluffy.

■ When the cakes are completely cool, use the filling and two cakes to make sandwiches.

JEFF SCHER

Beatrice's Chocolate Whoopie Pies

The following recipe is a favorite of the staff at Down East because Beatrice's daughter Linda brings them in to share. This version of the classic whoopie pie is moister than most and not as puffy. You'll gobble them up so fast you won't believe it.

Yield: 2 dozen small whoopie pies (about 2" diameter)

LINDA CALLAHAN

Cakes

½ cup dark cocoa powder

1 cup sugar

½ cup vegetable oil

1 egg

1 cup milk

1 teaspoon vanilla

1½ cups flour

1½ teaspoons baking soda

½ teaspoon baking powder

½ teaspoon salt

Filling

2 cups confectioners' sugar, sifted

1 cup salted butter, softened but not melted

2 teaspoons vanilla

½ cup Marshmallow Fluff

pinch of salt (optional)

- Preheat the oven to 425°F.
- In a large bowl mix together the cocoa powder and sugar. Stir in the oil, egg, milk, and vanilla. In a separate bowl stir together the flour, baking soda, baking powder, and salt. Mix the dry ingredients into the cocoa mixture.
- Drop the batter by small spoonfuls onto a parchment-lined baking sheet and bake for approximately 8 minutes. Remove to a rack to cool.
- Prepare filling by stirring the softened butter into the confectioners' sugar. Stir in the vanilla, Marshmallow Fluff, and optional salt. To assemble, spread a generous amount of filling on the flat side of one cake and top with a second cake.

" I remember Nana's whoopie pies being THE dessert at family cookouts," recalls Suzanne Conlon, Beatrice's granddaughter. "In fact, I don't ever remember eating them indoors. They seemed to be a summertime item, the seasonal counterpoint to caramels at Christmas. To this day, when I think of whoopie pies, I'm back at 55 Linden Street taking off the top and licking the icing. Hand-held cake—it's genius. "

The Eastwind Inn Whoopie Pies

Tim Watts, an avid baker since childhood, grew up with the whoopie pies his grandmother and mother baked at home in Tenants Harbor, Maine. In 1975, he bought, refurbished, and reopened the Eastwind Inn on the harbor's edge, a stone's throw from his family home. What's unusual about this third-generation whoopie pie baker and consumer is that when he decided to bake the dessert commercially, he borrowed a recipe from a family friend rather than using the one favored by his mother and grandmother. (Nothing against their recipe, he insists, but he prefers Brenda Scaccia's traditional Maine whoopie pie recipe, and he's been using it for many years now.)

Yield: 9 to 12 whoopies

Cakes

½ cup vegetable shortening

1 cup sugar

2 egg yolks

1 teaspoon vanilla

2 cups flour

5 tablespoons cocoa powder

1 teaspoon baking powder

1 teaspoon salt

1 cup milk

Filling

½ cup vegetable shortening

pinch of salt

2 cups confectioners' sugar

2 egg whites, beaten stiff

JEFF SCHER

■ Preheat the oven to 350°F.

■ In a large bowl cream together the shortening and sugar. Add the egg yolks and vanilla and mix again.

■ In a separate bowl blend the dry ingredients together. Add the dry ingredients to the creamed mixture alternately with the milk.

■ Drop the batter onto a cookie sheet with a medium-size ice cream scoop and bake for 12 to 15 minutes.

■ To make the filling: Blend the shortening, salt, and sugar. Once mixed, add the beaten egg whites.

■ When the cakes have cooled, spread a scoop of filling on one cake and top with another cake. Chill the assembled whoopies in the refrigerator to set up the filling.

■ If not to be served immediately, wrap individually in plastic and refrigerate.

Grandma Jenny's Maine Whoopie Pies

Jenny Jandreau is one of the reasons whoopie pies are gaining in popularity far beyond the Northeast. She's a native of Fort Kent, Maine, near the Canadian border, and comes from a big Franco-American family in a strong Franco-American community. She grew up with whoopie pies and has been eating and making them all her life. ¶ In 1992 Jenny moved to Arizona, where the whoopie pie is virtually unknown. That is, it was unknown until she arrived and began making them for her neighbors.

Yield: 12 whoopie pies

Filling

½ cup milk

2½ tablespoons flour

pinch of salt

¾ cup powdered sugar

½ cup vegetable shortening

1 teaspoon vanilla

Cakes

1½ cups sugar

½ cup vegetable shortening

2 eggs

1 teaspoon vanilla

1 cup sour cream

⅓ cup hot water

3¼ cups flour

1 teaspoon baking soda

1 teaspoon baking powder

½ teaspoon salt

½ cup Hershey cocoa

Recipe Notes from Grandma Jenny:

Remind children and hubby not to touch until after dinnertime!

Whoopie pies can be stored in sealed containers and left out on counter for about five days, or, if you prefer, they can also be refrigerated. You can also freeze them for later. We eat them so fast there are never any left after five days.

The filling can also be made with peanut butter. (We tested this ingredient a couple years ago, and it is my kids' favorite.) Simply add peanut butter to taste as last ingredient in the filling mixture and stir well to get the right consistency.

For this recipe, you make the filling first.

■ In a one- or two-quart saucepan heat over low to medium heat (to avoid burning or sticking) the milk, flour, and salt, stirring continuously until a paste is formed. Transfer paste into a bowl and refrigerate.

■ In a large bowl combine the powdered sugar, shortening, and vanilla and mix well. (For best blending results, use a mixer.)

■ Combine the chilled paste with the sugar and shortening mixture. Blend well, using a mixer.

Your tasty filling is complete!

■ When you are ready to bake the cakes, preheat the oven to 350°F.

■ Combine the sugar, shortening, eggs, vanilla, sour cream, and hot water and beat well.

■ In a separate bowl stir together the flour, baking soda, baking powder, salt and cocoa. Mix the dry and wet ingredients, then stir well. (The batter will be quite thick. If you are making a huge batch, as Jenny does, you may want to mix up the batter in several bowls.)

Now it's time for cooking!

■ Place rounded teaspoons of batter onto ungreased cookie sheets (8 to 12 per sheet). Wet a small spoon with water and go over each mound of batter to flatten it slightly and make a nice round shape.

■ Bake for 10 minutes. Place a large strip of wax paper on your countertop or kitchen table. Cool cakes slightly on the baking sheet, then place the completed whoopie rounds onto the wax paper.

■ Take two whoopie rounds, add desired amount of filling, put them together, and you're done. Enjoy!

"Confidential Chat" Boston Whoopie Pies

Diane Ward Harting comes from a Maine family, but she grew up in Boston, and says she remembers whoopie pies from Boston as well as from her summers in Turner, Maine. When she married in 1962, she was given a copy of the *Boston Globe's Cookbook for Brides* and began using the whoopie pie recipe she found there. Over the years, she's adapted it. ¶Most recipes in the *Boston Globe* newspaper and its cookbook were taken from the paper's "Confidential Chat" pages, a feature that ran for 128 years. People wrote in to ask each other questions and to seek recipes, but never used their real names. The same thing happens now on Internet blogs. ¶"Confidential Chat" turned out to be the longest-running feature in the *Globe*. Starting in 1884 as the "Housekeeper's Column," it was renamed "Confidential Chat" in 1922 and ran every Sunday until January, 2006. A *Globe* historian called it "the first regular column about women's affairs in any newspaper." ¶The whoopie pie recipe chosen for the *Globe* cookbook came from a contributor identified as "The Beachcomber," who commented, "This is quick and easy to make. Good for snacks. We love 'em for picnics." ¶This one has oil in the cake, margarine and Fluff in the filling.

Yield: 8 to 12 whoopies

Cakes

2 cups unsifted flour
1 teaspoon baking soda
¼ teaspoon salt
⅓ cup cocoa powder
1 cup sugar
1 egg
⅓ cup salad oil
1 teaspoon vanilla
¾ cup milk

Filling

1 stick margarine
1 cup confectioners' sugar
3 heaping tablespoons Marshmallow Fluff
1 teaspoon vanilla

■ Mix together first five ingredients. Then add remaining ingredients. Beat all together.

■ Drop by tablespoon onto greased cookie sheet, leaving space for each to spread as it bakes. Bake in 350°F oven for 12 minutes.

■ Beat together the filling ingredients and spread between cooled cakes.

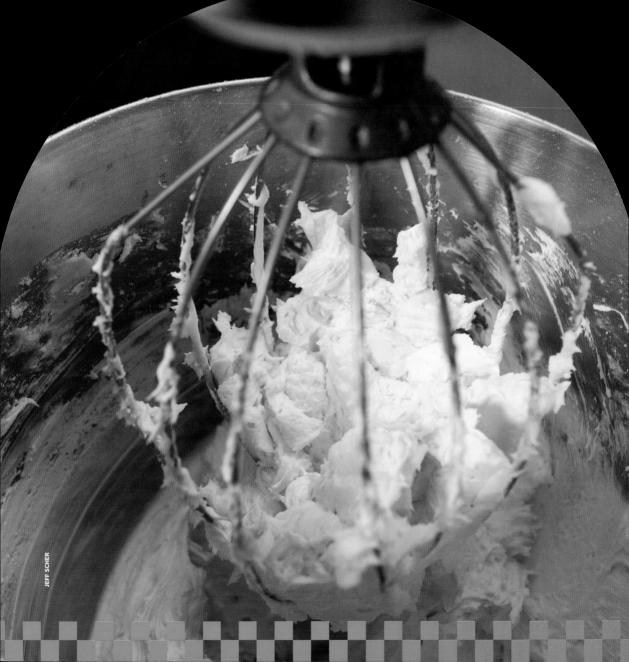

Diane's Modified Boston Globe Whoopie Pies

This adapted version of the preceding recipe replaces the margarine in the filling with a combination of cream cheese and butter, increases the cocoa, and reduces baking time for the cakes. After years of experimenting, Diane determined that her family likes this recipe best.

Yield: 8 to 12 whoopies

Cakes

2 cups unsifted flour

1 teaspoon baking soda

¼ teaspoon salt

½ cup unsweetened cocoa powder

1 cup sugar

1 egg

⅓ cup salad oil

1 teaspoon vanilla

¾ cup milk (Diane uses undiluted evaporated milk)

Filling

4 tablespoons butter

3 to 4 ounces cream cheese

1 cup confectioners' sugar

3 heaping tablespoons Marshmallow Fluff

1 teaspoon vanilla

■ Preheat oven to 350°F.

■ Mix together the flour, baking soda, salt, cocoa, and sugar. Add the egg, oil, vanilla, and milk and beat.

■ Drop the batter onto greased cookie sheets, leaving space for each to spread as it bakes. Bake for 8 minutes. Cool cakes on the pan briefly, then on a wire rack.

■ Beat together the butter, cream cheese, confectioners' sugar, Fluff, and vanilla and spread between cooled cakes.

Zingerman's BakehouseWhoopie Pies

Whoopie pie baker Amy Emberling, a native of Cape Breton, Nova Scotia, fondly recalls eating Vachon's famous Jos. Louis cakes of her youth "by the boxful." Colloquially called Joe Louises, they have been Canada's most popular snack cake for seventy-five years. They resemble moon pies on the outside, since they are flat and each cake is coated in chocolate. But fundamentally they're devil's food cake with a white, creamy filling, and not as lavishly filled as a regular whoopie pie. Emberling's love of these cakes, and chocolate in general, led her to develop a good whoopie pie recipe at her Zingerman's Bakehouse in Ann Arbor, Michigan. This recipe accompanied a *New York Times* March 17, 2009, article about the soaring popularity of whoopie pies.

Yield: 6 large whoopie pies

Cakes

¼ pound (1 stick) butter, at room temperature

1 cup light brown sugar

1 large egg

1 teaspoon vanilla extract

1¼ teaspoons baking soda

1 teaspoon sea salt

2 cups all-purpose flour

½ cup cocoa powder

1 cup buttermilk

Filling

3 large egg whites

¾ cup sugar

½ pound butter (2 sticks), at room temperature

¾ teaspoon vanilla extract

¼ teaspoon sea salt

For cakes:

■ Preheat the oven to 350°F.

■ In a mixing bowl, cream together the butter and brown sugar. Beat in the egg and vanilla until light and creamy.

■ In another bowl, whisk together the baking soda, salt, flour, and cocoa. Add the butter mixture in three parts, alternating with buttermilk. Combine well after each addition.

■ Use an ice cream scoop or a spoon to scoop out twelve ¼ cup mounds of batter. Place about 6 inches apart on a parchment-lined baking sheet.

■ Bake until the tops are puffed and cakes spring back when touched, 12 to 14 minutes. Remove cakes from oven, place on racks, and cool completely before filling.

For buttercream filling: For best results, pay attention to required temperatures.

■ Fill the bottom half of a double boiler (or a medium saucepan) with an inch or two of water, and bring to a simmer over high heat.

■ In the top half of the double boiler (or a metal bowl set over the hot water in the saucepan), combine egg whites and sugar. Whisk only until the sugar is dissolved and the temperature of the mixture reaches 180°F on an instant-read thermometer.

■ Remove from heat.

■ Using the whisk attachment on a heavy-duty mixer, whisk egg whites and sugar on high until doubled in volume, thick, and shiny. (Continue whisking until cool.)

■ Reduce speed to medium and start adding butter about ½ tablespoon at a time, until all butter is incorporated.

■ Add vanilla and salt. If the mixture looks curdled, continue to whisk until it becomes smooth again.

■ Increase speed to high and whisk 1 more minute.

■ Use the filling immediately or place in an airtight container and chill for up to 3 days, whisking again before using.

To assemble:

■ With an ice cream scoop or spoon, place ¼ cup filling on flat side of each of 6 cakes, spreading to edges. Top the filled half with another cake.

■ Store whoopie pies in an airtight container at room temperature for up to 3 days, or wrap individually and freeze for up to 3 months.

Two Fat Cats Bakery Whoopie Pies

"Within the first month, we were making whoopie pies," recalls Kristen DuShane, describing how she opened her Two Fat Cats Bakery in Portland, Maine, in 2005. After working for ten years in a number of restaurants "for some very talented people" she gravitated back to her first love, pastry, and decided to open her own little bakery, naming it for her two big fat orange cats whose pictures adorn a shelf in the shop. Her whoopies are of the marshmallow-crème variety, but with a twist: she makes the marshmallow crème herself. This recipe, adapted for the home baker, uses Marshmallow Fluff for the sake of simplicity.

Yield: 38 whoopie pies

Cakes

5¼ cups flour

⅞ cup cocoa powder (Dutch processed)

1 tablespoon baking powder

1 tablespoon baking soda

1 tablespoon salt

1½ sticks unsalted butter

2½ cups dark brown sugar

⅔ cup vegetable or canola oil

6 eggs

8 ounces bittersweet chocolate, melted and cooled

3 cups buttermilk

Filling

1 pound unsalted butter

1 cup confectioners' sugar, sifted

1 pound (the large container) Marshmallow Fluff

NANCY GRIFFIN

- Sift and whisk the flour, cocoa, baking powder, baking soda, and salt together.
- In a separate bowl cream the butter and sugar until the lumps are gone. Then drizzle in the oil. Add the eggs one at a time and beat together with a paddle attachment on a mixer until light brown. Scrape the bowl between additions. Add the melted chocolate and mix until combined.
- Preheat the oven to 350°F.
- Add the dry mixture and buttermilk alternately, beginning and ending with dry and scraping the bowl between additions.
- Pour the batter into a shallow container and chill for at least an hour before scooping and baking. Scoop batter onto a lightly greased or parchment-lined baking sheet and let rest 10 minutes before baking.
- Bake for 6 minutes, rotate, and then bake for another 6 to 7 minutes.
- To make the filling, using the mixer's paddle attachment, beat the butter and sugar together until light and fluffy. Add Marshmallow Fluff and continue to beat until thoroughly incorporated.
- Filling can be kept in the refrigerator for up to a week or frozen for a month. To re-beat, bring up to room temperature and whip with whisk attachment.
- Assemble whoopie pies once cakes are completly cooled.

"Nobody can pinpoint the reason the whoopie pie finally broke into the national consciousness. But the snacks evoke a more homespun era that seems to provide some comfort. 'Pure edible nostalgia' the Williams-Sonoma catalog calls them."

—"Whoopie! Cookie, Pie, or Cake, It's Having Its Moment," *New York Times*, March 17, 2009

Getting Whoopies

If you live in Maine or Pennsylvania and you don't want to make whoopies, getting a whoopie pie is as easy as, well, pie.

Go to any big supermarket bakery department, or head for the little grocery or convenience store down the street, where you'll undoubtedly find them near the register, in a plastic wrapper, selling for two dollars, give or take.

Both states have bakeries and restaurants where whoopies are available in the case and on the menu. Whoopies can also be found at farmers' markets and upscale bakeries, the latter often offering whoopies that differ in flavors, sizes, and even shapes from the traditional varieties. Even at small-town bakeries where the standard whoopie may dominate, these days it's rarely the only flavor choice.

Things are looking up in other parts of the country, and even outside of the country. Some nationwide retail chains such as Trader Joe's and Whole Foods sell whoopie pies, as do many regional chains, even

JEFF SCHER

in regions where whoopie pies were unknown as recently as a decade ago.

In New York City, several topnotch bakeries now offer elegant whoopie pies with adult filling flavors such as espresso, but these fancy confections are still whoopie pies, still that easy-to-eat finger food. New York's Magnolia Bakery, made famous for its cupcakes on the HBO series *Sex and the City*, has recently taken to selling whoopies. The pumpkin whoopie recipe from Matt Lewis of Baked, a Brooklyn bakery, is available on the Martha Stewart Web site.

An upscale Boston restaurant, Finale, which, as its name indicates, is devoted to desserts, serves mini-whoopies alongside its handmade ice creams.

But this is the twenty-first century, and you don't have to travel to Maine or Lancaster County or the megalopolis for your whoopie fix. Now whoopie lovers everywhere can sit at their computer anywhere and order whoopie pies over the Internet. Not only do many of the commercial bakers encourage online orders, but the snacks are also available on eBay and amazon.com and from catalog retailers such as the Vermont Country Store and Williams-Sonoma. Or you can cheat and order the mix from Stonewall Kitchen and make whoopies of your own.

It's a brave new whoopie world.

WHOOPIE WISDOM

ENERGY BOOSTS

Chef-instructor Howard "Corky" Clark runs the seafood kitchen for the Culinary Institute of America in Hyde Park, New York. He and his wife, Nancy, grew up in Pennsylvania Dutch country, and he recalls how the farm kids there would eat huge breakfasts early in the morning to provide lots of calories for days of hard work in the fields with their families. When the midmorning slump hit, whoopie pies were one of the high-carbohydrate snacks dispensed for that extra burst of energy that would carry the young field hands to lunchtime.

JEFF SCHER

✳ Who's Who of Whoopies

There are whoopie wondermen and women all over the country (and the world) these days. And while most whoopie bakers reside in Maine and Pennsylvania, there is a growing contingent hitting urban areas and rural outposts alike. Here we take a look at some of the kings and queens of the whoopie world—plus some completely random but interesting whoopie pie makers who prove you never know just where you might encounter a wonderful whoopie.

Upper Crust

Nina Stoltzfus grew up in Indiana with a Mennonite mom and an Amish dad. "It was a big Amish community," she explains, and her mother regularly made whoopie pies, as did Nina when she grew big enough.

Since 2002, she's operated her own Upper Crust Bakery in Amish country, Leola, Pennsylvania. Here she bakes forty dozen whoopie pies at a time, in five varieties, and sells them in the bakery, wholesales

COURTESY SHEETZ, INC

them to restaurants, and ships them out to fill mail orders.

Stoltzfus uses her family recipe with a vegetable shortening filling for the traditional chocolate whoopie and the chocolate with peanut butter version. For her red velvet, vanilla with chocolate chip, and vanilla with raspberry whoopies, however, she switches to a buttercream filling.

"I started out working in a bakery in Lancaster that used whipped cream to fill their whoopie pies," says Stoltzfus. "That's just not right!"

Gobs and Gobbz of Whoopies

Sheetz is a family-owned chain of 350 gas stations and convenience stores with restaurants offering espresso and made-to-order food. Based in Altoona, Pennsylvania, the chain started in 1952 when Bob Sheetz bought one of his father's five dairy stores. Today Sheetz gas stations sell biofuels and Sheetz restaurants sell whoopie pies. Except they call them gobs, or, in their case, Gobbz—Sheetz marketing efforts have long capitalized on that Z in the family name.

However, Sheetz, like many other convenience store chains, doesn't make their own baked goods. Their Gobbz are made by Shirley's Cookies, in Claysburg, Pennsylvania, which bakes private-label items for several customers.

Shirley's began baking whoopie pies in 2004 for a customer who just didn't want to keep making them. "We made up our own recipe," explains Patty Shaw, sales manager. These days Shirley's bakes four flavors—traditional chocolate, chocolate with peanut butter filling, red velvet with white filling, and pumpkin with white filling—and none of them contains any marshmallow or cream cheese. And while Sheetz calls them Gobbz, Shirley's calls them whoopie pies. Gobs "is a central Pennsylvania term," says Shaw.

ISAMAX SNACKS BAKERY

Queen of Whoopies

Amy Bouchard is called the Queen of the Whoopie Pie in Maine, partly because she skyrocketed into the national consciousness when she appeared on the QVC shopping channel with her Maine-made whoopie pies and caused a sensation.

And that was nothing compared to the Oprah factor. When Oprah decided Amy's whoopie pies were the best she'd ever tasted, life changed permanently for the Isamax Snacks Bakery in Gardiner, Maine.

Amy Bouchard started out, like many other

> **"There's nothing foo-foo about whoopie pies. They're fun,"** declares Amy Bouchard. **"When I first went on QVC, no one knew anything about whoopie pies. They make you feel like a kid again, even if you never had one as a kid. They remind you of your grandmother, even if she didn't make them!"**

Bouchard makes fourteen regular whoopie pie flavors for wholesale, including mint, gingerbread, red velvet, vanilla bean, banana crème, Chocolate Lovers, chocolate chip, maple, oatmeal cream, peanut butter, pumpkin, raspberry and cream, and strawberry. In addition, she makes orange and lemon mini whoopies, and a couple of Whoop-de-Doos (whoopie pies dipped all over in chocolate).

young mothers, looking for something she could do to bring in a little money when her two children were tiny. She loved to bake, so she began making whoopie pies and selling them locally. On a big day, she might make a dozen. Then, carrying her smallest child, Isabella, in one arm and a basket of whoopie pies in the other, Amy would make her rounds.

After a year or so, when Isabella was a full-fledged toddler, Amy put her down in a little convenience store–restaurant one day while she arranged her whoopie pie display. Isabella gleefully proceeded to squash all the potato chip bags and then sat herself down at a nearby table beside an older man who she seemed to think needed help eating his meal.

Time for day care, thought Amy.

Now Bouchard's "rounds" take her to food trade shows and conferences all across the country, where as many as fifty thousand people have the opportunity to try one of her Wicked Whoopies. *Phantom Gourmet*, a Boston-based TV and radio show that produces food events and also rates restaurants and food purveyors, deemed Amy's the "World's Greatest Whoopie Pie" for five years in a row, making Wicked Whoopies one of their "Great Eight."

Isamax Snacks Bakery was named for Amy's two children, Isabella and Maxx. Maxx works full-time in the business now, as does her husband, David. Isabella helps out after school and in the summer.

Today Isamax makes an average of four thousand Wicked Whoopies a day at a new bakery facility in Gardiner, not too far from the first little whoopie pie shop Amy opened in 2003—which was probably the first whoopie pie shop in the world. She now has two other outlets, in Farmingdale and Freeport, Maine.

Bouchard's first shop had been open only a few months when Oprah called—one of her producers had seen it while vacationing in Maine.

"I was freaking out" when the fateful call came through, Bouchard admits. The editors from *O, the Oprah* magazine, warned her she might be deluged with orders when the issue featuring Wicked Whoopies hit the newsstands. "I didn't even have a Web site!" Amy exclaims. "I'd never done mail order." All that soon changed, and deluged she was. Still is. The magazine article ran in December 2003, and an *O* editor brought them to the TV show as one of his favorite gifts for that season. The calls are still coming in.

WHOOPIE WISDOM

WICKED

"In Maine," says Amy Bouchard of Wicked Whoopies, "when something is good, we call it 'good.' When something is great, we call it 'wicked.'"

Despite the size of her bakery's business today, Bouchard still takes mail orders personally and still shops for special cards to enclose with a handwritten greeting to mark whatever the occasion—birthdays, graduations, friendship. One of her mottos is "making smiles every day."

Back when she launched her baking career, Amy chose whoopie pies simply because she loved them, and she still does. She uses the same recipe she used when she was sixteen, although she confesses she's tweaked it a bit. She now produces fourteen flavors regularly for her wholesale trade, but in her retail shops, she says, she continues to try out new combinations. "I came out with all the flavors because I want to make everyone happy."

La- Whoopie Kings

Amy Bouchard may be the queen of Maine whoopie pies, but Bernie LaBree is surely the king. LaBree's Bakery in Old Town, Maine, turns out several million whoopie pies annually, and in 2009 made plans to expand the operation to triple the output.

Bernie's father and uncle opened the bakery in 1948, and now his son has joined the business. LaBree's has been baking whoopie pies since the 1960s, as near as Bernie can recall.

COURTESY LABRE'S BAKERY

Fabian Labadie

NANCY GRIFFIN

The bakery ships its products all over the United States and into Canada. With the expansion, LaBree expects to branch out to Mexico and perhaps even as far away as Dubai.

LaBree's sells a lot of private-label whoopie pies to supermarkets—such as six-packs of juniors and shells for retailers to fill themselves. The company sticks primarily to five varieties: the conventional chocolate with white or peanut butter filling, and three with a cream cheese–based filling—red velvet, carrot, and pumpkin. A special request from a Detroit customer prompted development of a banana whoopie with a banana and marshmallow filling.

Another giant among whoopie makers in the Pine Tree State is Labadie's Bakery in Lewiston, which also bakes thousands of the pies every week. Theirs are made with a vegetable shortening–based filling. Many are sold to private-label customers and some go to retail outlets under the Labadie's name, but many whoopie pie lovers insist on getting their treats directly from Labadie's no-frills outlet store in the heart of the city's Franco-American community, where it's been a fixture for generations.

Fabian Labadie is the current owner of the family business, which began in 1918. Oral tradition holds that Labadie's has been selling

DAWNA HILTON

NANCY GRIFFIN

whoopie pies since 1925, but unfortunately a fire in 1967—before Fabian worked there—wiped out all records, so the venerable bakery can't unequivocally claim to be the first to make whoopie pies.

Holy Whoopies!

Downtown Bangor, Maine, may lay claim to the most interesting whoopie pie bakery of all: The Friars' Bakehouse. It's a tiny storefront filled with statues of saints and religious pictures, presided over by two men in brown, cowled robes who serve the public from behind a glass case filled with bread, cookies, and delectable (dare we say "divine"?) whoopie pies. It's no gimmick. They're really Franciscan Brothers of St. Elizabeth of Hungary. This is probably the only whoopie pie bakery in the world with a Latin motto: *Ad Majorem Dei Gloriam.*

Brothers Don and Ken started out in 1995 by hand-cranking bread dough in a galvanized bread bucket, and selling the loaves to local people. Today the old hand-cranked bucket sits on the counter with a sign reading "Donations."

"We made thousands of loaves in that old bucket," says Brother Ken. After a couple of years they found the storefront, opened their little cafe with a couple of tables, and expanded from making just bread to offering a whole line of baked goods, including whoopie pies.

The whoopie pies are a big seller as a snack with coffee, a dessert for luncheon diners, and as a takeout six-pack in a plastic bag. The brothers bake three hundred whoopie pies a day, which usually sell out by closing time. In the summer, when tourists visit the Queen City, the Friars' Bakehouse whoopie pies may all be gone by noon.

Brother Ken doesn't give out the bakehouse recipe, because, as he puts it, "It's our livelihood." But he does acknowledge that the filling for his traditional whoopie pie falls squarely in the "no marshmallow" column. You might say he's a purist.

Portland Pies

While most of the whoopie pies sold at Maine convenience stores and takeout shops are baked by one of the bigger bakeries and sold under the store's private label, that's not the case at Anania's in Portland.

Anania's is a three-store, family-owned grocery and Italian takeout-food chain in Maine's largest city, and for twenty years the shops have been selling whoopies made by Barbara Anania.

A Portland native, she grew up eating whoopie pies, so years later, when she decided to stop working as a nurse in order to spend more time with her

WHOOPIE WISDOM

MINI ME WHOOPIES

"My mother-in-law told me they always made minis of the Italian treats," Barbara Anania explains, "so I tried minis, too, and they were a big hit." The less-than-two-inch minis are strategically placed near the checkout at Anania's, where they are scooped up constantly. "I guess they're more guilt-free," suggests Barbara.

three small children and help out the family business, her thoughts naturally turned to whoopies. She tried out and tweaked a number of recipes before she found one that was not too sweet and provided good consistency for production. It proved so popular that she launched her Sweets and Treats bakery, making whoopie pies for Anania's and initially selling some wholesale.

Time constraints meant she had to give up selling her whoopies wholesale, but they are now also available through the family catering business, as are large whoopie pie cakes, which she's been making for twenty years.

When she began, Barbara made traditional whoopie pies only. Then she added one with a peanut butter filling. Now she also offers oatmeal and chocolate chip varieties. "I don't consider those whoopie pies," she says, "but the customers do."

Mains's Maine Whoopies

When people find a whoopie pie they love, they'll travel almost any distance to get it, no matter how small or remote the bakery.

That's the case with MainSweets bakery, named for owner Patty Mains, located 6.2 miles off U.S. Route 1, down a gorgeous coastal peninsula in tiny Five Islands, Maine.

Everything made at MaineSweets is old-fashioned—whoopie pies, date squares, Needham candies, lemon bars. Mains gets up really early to bake the bread and sweets fresh daily. She says she doesn't know exactly when her late grandmother began using the whoopie pie recipe (with no Marshmallow Fluff) that Mains swears by, but it's been a while— her grandmother was born in 1892.

Regular summer visitors from all over make a beeline to MainSweets the minute they arrive in the area, and often as not they vie with all the locals who make several trips a week to stock up on whoopie pies.

NANCY GRIFFIN

Farm Whoopies

In Turner, Maine, a family farm is turning into a destination for everything homegrown and whole-some—from alpaca fleece to whoopie pies. At Nez-inscot Farm, named for the nearby river, Gloria Varney's been baking whoopie pies since she opened the farm store twenty years ago. Her mother and grandmother made whoopies, and she still uses their recipe to make the cake (minus the red food coloring they used to put in the batter).

"I changed the filling, too," Gloria explains. "Ours has butter and cream cheese, lightened up. There are only four ingredients in it." They're good ingredients, too, since Varney and her family raise the cows that provide the organic milk and butter.

A firm believer that people should know the source of their food, she earned her degree in community health education, originally intend-ing to work in a health-care facility. Then she and her husband bought his family's 250-acre farm in 1987. After a few years working off the farm, Varney realized that promoting a healthy lifestyle and educating people through growing and selling fresh, nutritious products from the farm worked better for her, and might actually be more effective as well in getting the word out about sensible nutrition.

Beep's Whoopies

Beep's Bakery in Sumner, Maine, got its name be-cause Beeps is what Glenn Hinckley's first grandchild called him. Rev. Hinckley and his wife, Rev. Linda Smith, combine an interesting set of careers. These ordained ministers bake bread and sweet things, and also practice Integrated Energy Therapy under the business name of Two Spirits Healing. They es-pouse a healthy lifestyle, but clearly don't exclude treats. They make all their baked goods with natural and local ingredients, when possible, including bak-ing powder that contains no aluminum.

It all started with donuts. Glenn is a dedicated donut maker who was encouraged by friends to

make them commercially, and when he decided to give it a try, Linda thought she might as well contribute to the enterprise with her own favorite baked good, the whoopie pie.

"I grew up with the almond variety—my mother and grandmother made them," says Linda. They always added almond flavoring to the vanilla buttercream filling, she explains, "and as far as I knew growing up, that was a whoopie pie." When she started making them for the bakery, though, she learned local people didn't like

their whoopie pies with almond filling. It's still her favorite, but her biggest seller is the classic plain vanilla filled whoopie.

She makes a white, cooked filling with a little flour, milk, butter, and granulated sugar. Her mother alternated between the two traditional fillings—one with vegetable shortening and one with Marshmallow Fluff.

Standard Beep's filling flavors are vanilla, almond, peanut butter, coffee, raspberry, and pumpkin with cream cheese, and sometimes peppermint.

Not Noticeably Nutritious:

RecipeZaar.com, a popular recipe Web site, calculates that the number of calories in their "Whoopie Pies—the Real Deal—Lancaster Co. Recipe" totals approximately 518 per pie. The breakdown is about 4 grams of protein, 59 grams of carbohydrates, and 30 grams of fat. (Just for some perspective, a large Vanilla Bean Coolatta from Dunkin' Donuts contains more than 800 calories, while a Snickers bar contains about 271 calories.)

JEFF SCHER

Healthy Whoopies

Whoopie pies were never intended to be health food, although some apologists may point out that dark chocolate is thought to be therapeutic for depression and contains useful antioxidants. If you are good at stretching a nutritional point to near-breaking, you could also argue that the whoopie pies with cream cheese–based fillings offer some calcium and a bit of protein. And, after all, there are eggs in the cake.

Those who are left unswayed by such rationalizations, but who want to have their cake and eat it, too, preferably without the full measure of guilt, will long for a healthier version of this unashamedly rich dessert. Also, some people's bodies just can't tolerate certain ingredients, so for those watching their cholesterol or weight, or those allergic folks who suffer whoopie pie deprivation not of their own choosing—help is on the way. Here you'll find two recipes that attempt to wholesome-up the whoopie.

Cake and Commerce's
Gluten-Free Whoopie Pies

When a nutritionist told Linsey Herman, proprietor of the Cake and Commerce Web site, **www.cakeandcommerce.com**, to try a gluten-free diet to help alleviate some symptoms of a chronic illness, she naturally had to find a way to make a whoopie pie that met the gluten-free standard but also still tasted like a real whoopie pie. Before developing her gluten-free recipe, Herman experimented with regular wheat flour recipes to find the standard she wanted to reach, ending up with a Mennonite recipe as a baseline. ¶While Herman doesn't think her recipe is a perfect replication of the wheat flour original, she does report that her mother ate most of one without realizing it was gluten-free. When she made the discovery, she kept right on eating.

Yield: Approximately 12 whoopie pies

Cakes

¾ teaspoon salt

1½ teaspoons baking powder

½ teaspoon baking soda

¼ cup + 2 tablespoons tapioca flour

1½ cups light buckwheat flour

½ cup cocoa powder

½ cup almond flour (as fresh as possible—grind your own if possible)

2 tablespoons rice flour

2 teaspoons guar gum (optional—if you don't use it, your pies will spread out more)

4 ounces (1 stick) butter

1 cup sugar

1 egg + 1 egg yolk

1 cup buttermilk

1 teaspoon vanilla extract

Filling

4 ounces (1 stick) butter

¾ cup confectioners' sugar

¼ cup buttermilk

¼ teaspoon salt (dissolve in buttermilk, if possible)

½ to1 teaspoon vanilla extract (depending on how much vanilla flavor you want)

In this recipe Hermans uses a lot of light buckwheat and tapioca flour, and, to keep the cakes from spreading during baking, she adds some guar gum. Some alternatives: gluten-free oat flour (its strong taste limits the uses for Herman), whole-ground teff flour (used in Ethiopian injera fermented bread), garbanzo flour (in small quantities) and arrowroot (as a thickener).

■ Preheat the oven to 350° F.

■ Sift salt, baking powder, baking soda, tapioca flour, buckwheat flour, cocoa, almond flour, rice flour, and guar gum together. Mix the sugar and butter until fluffy. Add eggs and mix until combined. Alternate additions of dry ingredients and buttermilk and vanilla, until everything is in the mixing bowl. Mix briefly, until all ingredients are evenly and thoroughly combined. Make sure batter is fairly firm—it should not be wet or gooey.

■ Using a small ice cream scoop, scoop balls of batter onto a parchment-lined baking sheet. Leave room for the balls to spread.

■ Bake for 10 to 15 minutes or until a toothpick comes out dry or the top of the cake does not retain a mark when touched. (For a slightly more fudgy cake, pull it out of the oven before the top feels firm.)

■ Cool completely before filling.

■ To make the filling, mix the butter and half the confectioners' sugar until it resembles corn meal. (If it combines completely, that's okay.) Add the buttermilk, salt, and vanilla. Mix until completely incorporated. Gradually add more confectioners' sugar until mixture is spreadable but stiff enough to hold its shape.

■ Apply filling using a pastry bag fitted with a star tip or a round tip to create a pretty pattern or just spread a dollop on the cookie with an offset spatula or anything handy you happen to have around your kitchen.

■ If you wrap the assembled whoopie pies in plastic, they will soften up. (Herman believes whoopie pies taste best when they are softer, after they've sat in plastic for a day.)

Davene's Zucchini Whoopie Pies

Another nutritionally reengineered whoopie comes from Davene Fahy, of Thomaston, Maine, who makes a zucchini whoopie pie from a recipe that replaces the butter in the cake with canola oil. The filling has cottage cheese whipped in to replace half the cream cheese, lowering the fat content even more. ¶ The texture of vegetable-based whoopie pie cakes can never resemble the high-fat cakes of a traditional whoopie pie, especially the chocolate ones, but better lowered-fat than no whoopie at all. Right?

Cakes

1 cup grated zucchini

¾ cup light brown sugar

½ cup canola oil

1 large egg

2 cups unbleached white flour

1 teaspoon baking soda

1 teaspoon baking powder

1 teaspoon cinnamon

½ teaspoon salt

½ teaspoon cloves

1 teaspoon vanilla

1 cup chopped nuts (optional)

Filling

4 ounces cream cheese, at room temperature

½ cup cottage cheese

2 teaspoons vanilla

1 cup confectioners' sugar, or more to taste

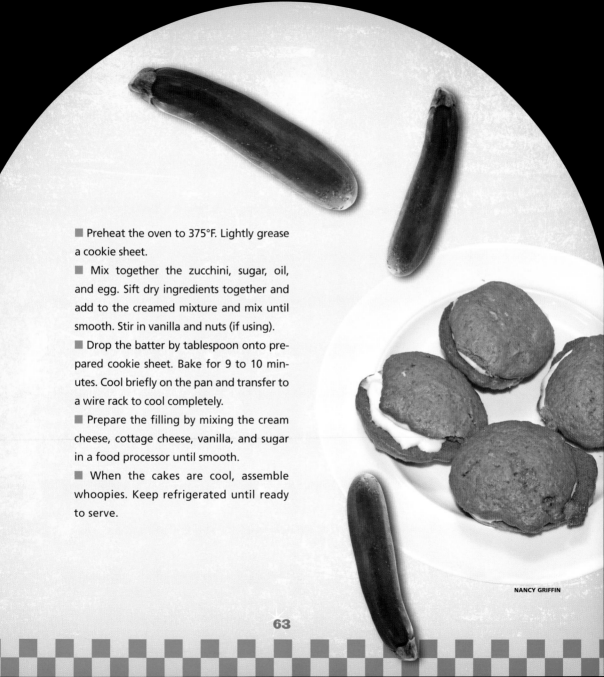

■ Preheat the oven to 375°F. Lightly grease a cookie sheet.

■ Mix together the zucchini, sugar, oil, and egg. Sift dry ingredients together and add to the creamed mixture and mix until smooth. Stir in vanilla and nuts (if using).

■ Drop the batter by tablespoon onto prepared cookie sheet. Bake for 9 to 10 minutes. Cool briefly on the pan and transfer to a wire rack to cool completely.

■ Prepare the filling by mixing the cream cheese, cottage cheese, vanilla, and sugar in a food processor until smooth.

■ When the cakes are cool, assemble whoopies. Keep refrigerated until ready to serve.

NANCY GRIFFIN

Another color, another shell
Another flavor that goes down well
A brand new fillin', it's oh, so thrillin',
Another whoopie!

—(To the tune of *Makin' Whoopee,* by Gus Kahn)

ISAMAX SNACKS BAKERY

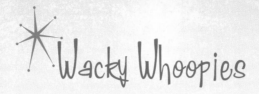 Wacky Whoopies

Perhaps the first radical change in the traditional whoopie pie was the peanut butter filling, or at least it was the first to catch on and skyrocket to popularity.

Some food historians, however, posit the idea that the molasses whoopie may have been the original, back in the days when rural folks had lots of molasses and little access to chocolate. And if that's the case, then the chocolate cakes would have been the first big change in the whoopie. But that's another story.

Most whoopie pie bakers now offer the peanut butter filling, and when they do, usually report it is their second-best selling variety. Recipes for traditional whoopie pies often include the peanut butter option as a variant to the white filling recipe.

If we accept chocolate as the original, in the evolution of the whoopie flavors, first came different fillings for chocolate pies, then bakers branched out to vanilla cakes with a variety of fillings. Then bits of things began creeping into the cakes and the fillings in the form of chips and fruits. The floodgates were opened.

Now, the sky's the limit.

FLAVOR FRENZY

The following flavors were all offered in 2008 at the fifth annual Pennsylvania Whoopie Pie Festival, at Hershey Farm in Ronks. In 2008 the farm was voted the number one whoopie pie (maker) in Lancaster County. Whoopie pies are the biggest-selling item available in the bakery, restaurant, farmers' markets, and online, though all the flavors below are not available year-round.

Chocolate shell with: regular peanut butter, vanilla, mint chip, raspberry, strawberry, cookies and cream, coffee, banana, chocolate, cream cheese, spice, and mint fillings

Pumpkin shell with: vanilla, cream cheese, and spice fillings

Red Velvet shell with: vanilla and cream cheese fillings

Vanilla shell with: regular, peanut butter, vanilla, mint chip, raspberry, strawberry, cookies and cream, coffee, banana, chocolate, cream cheese, spice, peanut butter and jelly, and lemon fillings

Orange shell with: vanilla and cream cheese fillings

Strawberry shell with: regular, vanilla, banana, chocolate, and cream cheese fillings

Peanut Butter shell with: regular, peanut butter, and chocolate fillings

Chocolate shell on top and Vanilla shell on bottom with: regular, peanut butter, vanilla, mint chop, raspberry, strawberry, cookies and cream, coffee, banana, chocolate, cream cheese, and spice fillings

Chocolate shell with candy filling: M&M, caramel, Heath Bar, malted milk balls, candy corn, Andes Candies, Reese's Pieces and peanuts

Caramel Apple Chocolate shell: with apples and caramel mixed in the filling

Hawaiian wedding: with pineapple pieces and coconut mixed in the filling

Peanut Butter/ Marshmallow shell with: peanut butter and marshmallow mixed in the filling

ISAMAX SNACKS BAKERY

Maine also has a festival to celebrate whoopie pies and their plentiful iterations. The first Maine Whoopie Pie Festival was held in Dover-Foxcroft in June 2009. One of the big winners was Betty Ree Zolla, who bakes her Betty Reez whoopie pies out of her Freeport, Maine, kitchen and sells them at several venues, including Good Eats Boutique in Portland. She won first prize in one of the judged categories and third in the other two—the only contestant to place in all three. She also tied for third in the People's Choice category.

Her first-place win was in the Most Original Whoopie Pie category, which she took with her Needham whoopie pie. Needhams are a traditional Maine candy featuring a potato and coconut filling wrapped in dark chocolate.

Other winners in the category, their flavors showing a definite Maine theme, were Cranberry Island Kitchen of Portland with a maple whoopie pie, and a Maine wild blueberry whoopie from Heather's Whoopie Pies in Lamoine.

Flavors other than traditional are so common now that the second category in the competition (after traditional, of course) was Best Flavored Whoopie Pie, which assumes certain flavors are accepted and not "original." Winning flavors were gingerbread-lemon, peanut butter, and almond.

WHOOPIE WISDOM

A PERFECT PAIR

Donna Carrigan, a kitchen designer from Walpole who entered the Maine Whoopie Pie Festival competition, posted a sign beside her coffee brandy whoopie pies that read "Maine's Favorites, Together at Last"—a tongue-in-cheek reference to the state's largest-selling liquor, Allen's Coffee Brandy.

Scores of Shapes

Flavor isn't the only thing changing in the world of whoopies. Shape is on the table, too.

Twenty years ago Carol Ford and Karen Haase began baking whoopie pies on Little Cranberry Island, three miles off the coast of Acadia National Park, and their efforts met with such success that they launched their business, Cranberry Island Kitchen, a few years ago. Sales were boosted by an appearance on the Martha Stewart TV show (the celebrity homemaker and Mount Desert Island summer resident declared their whoopies to be her favorite), mention in a *New York Times* article, and having their whoopie named the best in Maine by *Down East* magazine in 2008. Their heart-shaped version of the whoopie pie was featured in the Williams-Sonoma catalog. In 2009 the women moved their bakery to Portland, expanding to meet increased demand.

Their chocolate whoopie, while it comes with a traditional vanilla-flavored filling, is also available with such sophisticated filling flavors as Cointreau and orange zest, Myers Dark Rum, Chambord, and Champagne. Besides the liquor flavors (others may be substituted at the customer's request), other adult flavorings include freshly brewed espresso and rich chocolate. Another vanilla whoopie they offer is rolled in crushed peppermint candy.

One particularly unusual feature of the Cranberry Island whoopies is their shape. The chocolate pies are shaped like another Maine favorite, the mussel. The bivalve-shaped whoopie pies are sold in a little gingham-patterned open cardboard box wrapped in plastic. Their pumpkin whoopies are shaped like cute little pumpkins, while the vanilla whoopies have a scallop-shell shape.

All Cranberry Island Kitchen whoopies contain all-natural and organic local ingredients, including Kate's Homemade Butter, from a small family-owned Maine business. Although on their Web site, www.cranberryislandkitchen.com, Ford and Haase call their recipe secret, they did share it with Martha Stewart and it has appeared on her Web site.

Holiday Whoopies

Playing around with the shapes and flavors has led some home and commericial bakers to the realization that the whoopie pie can be tailored to just about any occasion. One Pennsylvania bakery put whoopies on the romantic holiday radar when they dyed the batter red and baked them in heart-shaped pans for Valentine's Day.

Located in Bird-in-Hand, Pennsylvania, population 300, nestled in the heart of Lancaster County's Pennsylvania Dutch country, the Bird-in-Hand Bakery has been producing whoopie pies since it opened a quarter-century ago.

"I grew up with them," says John Smucker, company CEO and a member of that famous jelly-making family. He was enjoying whoopie pies long before the bakery opened, since at least the 1950s, when they were made at home on the Smucker farm by his mother and by "Grussy," a.k.a. Grandma Smucker.

The family recipe, now the bakery recipe as well, calls for vegetable shortening and does not include marshmallow crème in the filling. In a unique little twist, though, this recipe adds some lemon flavoring along with the vanilla.

In 2008, Smucker sent a batch of the bakery's red velvet whoopie pies prepared in heart shapes to TV celebrity chef Rachael Ray. "I talked her into featuring them on her Valentine's Day show," he reports. They were a runaway hit. Now Bird-in-Hand bakes the heart-shaped confections every Valentine's Day, and offers other special holiday versions, such as green-colored mint filling for St. Patrick's Day.

Red Velvet Whoopie Pies

Red velvet whoopie pies are a popular variety at any time of year, not just for Valentine's Day. Here is one from Amy Bouchard of Isamax Snacks Bakery. This recipe gives a choice of fillings. For a less sweet filling, use the version with cream cheese.

Cakes

2 cups all-purpose flour

3 tablespoons cocoa powder

1 teaspoon baking soda

1 teaspoon salt

⅔ cup buttermilk (or ⅔ cup light cream mixed with 1 tablespoon vinegar)

2 teaspoons vanilla

¾ cup (1½ sticks) butter

1 cup granulated sugar

2 large eggs

2 ounces red food coloring

Basic marshmallow filling

6 heaping tablespoons Marshmallow Fluff

2 tablespoons vanilla

4 tablespoons flour

4 tablespoons milk

4 cups confectioners' sugar

1½ cups shortening

Filling with cream cheese

2 eight-ounce packages soft cream cheese

½ cup (1 stick) soft butter

2 cups confectioners' sugar

2 teaspoons vanilla

6 heaping tablespoons Marshmallow Fluff

■ Preheat the oven to 350°F.

■ Mix together the flour, cocoa, baking soda, and salt and set aside.

■ In a separate bowl, combine the buttermilk (or cream and vinegar) and vanilla.

■ Cream together the butter and sugar. Add the eggs and beat until fluffy. Stir in the dry ingredients, red food coloring, and cream mixture until well blended.

■ Drop the batter onto a greased or parchment-lined baking sheet with an ice cream scoop or tablespoon, spacing at least 2 inches apart.

■ Bake for 7 to 12 minutes, depending on the size of scoop you used. The cakes are done when the top springs back when gently touched. (You can also use a toothpick to check. When it comes out clean from the center, they are ready to come out of the oven.)

■ Make the filling of your choice by combining all ingredients and whipping until smooth.

■ When the cakes are completely cool, scoop the filling onto one whoopie cake, then place another cake on top (like a sandwich). Wrap in wax paper or plastic wrap to keep fresh.

King Arthur Flour's
Vanilla Berry Cream Whoopie Pies

King Arthur Flour is an employee-owned and -managed company in Norwich, Vermont. Founded in 1790, it is the oldest flour company in the United States (started when George Washington was in his first term). Frank Sands, of the founding family, instituted an employee stock-ownership program in 1996 and the employees now own 100 percent of the company, which is noted for its unbleached white flour and a catalog of baking products. It should come as no surprise that these dedicated workers happen to love whoopie pies, and some also love to make them and blog about them. King Arthur's bakers also offer a peanut butter whoopie pie in reverse—the peanut butter's in the cake and the filling is chocolate. Ah, the possibilities! ¶This recipe comes from baker and owner MaryJane Robbins, who says that "the Bakewell Cream really gives this batter extra loft, making for a nicely domed whoopie."

Yield: 8 to12 whoopies

Cakes

1 cup sugar

½ cup vegetable shortening

½ cup buttermilk, or soured milk

½ cup water

2 large eggs, room temperature, or ½ cup egg substitute, such as Egg Beaters

1 teaspoon vanilla extract

2¾ cups King Arthur All-Purpose Flour

1½ teaspoons Bakewell Cream

½ teaspoon baking soda

¼ teaspoon salt

Filling

1 cup vegetable shortening

1 cup confectioners' sugar

1⅓ cups Marshmallow Fluff

¼ teaspoon salt

1½ teaspoons vanilla extract

½ to ¾ cup of your favorite berry jam

additional fresh berries (optional)

Bakewell Cream, made in Hampden, Maine, for sixty years, is a powdered leavening agent that can be used in most recipes to replace baking powder or cream of tartar. The familiar bright yellow and blue eight-ounce canister has the company's famous "no fail" biscuit recipe printed on the back. It is sold mostly in Maine and some other New England outlets, and also available online from various suppliers.

■ Preheat the oven to 350°F. Line 2 baking sheets with parchment, or coat lightly with cooking spray.

■ Place the sugar and shortening in a mixer bowl and cream until light and fluffy.

■ To the creamed mixture, add the buttermilk and water and mix well. Add the eggs and vanilla. The mixture will look lumpy and curdled, but will come together when the dry ingredients are incorporated.

■ In a separate bowl, sift together the flour, Bakewell Cream, baking soda, and salt. Add to the wet ingredients and beat for one minute. Do not overmix or the cakes will be tough.

■ Using a tablespoon-size cookie scoop, place scoops of batter approximately 2 inches apart on the cookie sheets. You can bake right away for higher-domed cakes, or let sit 5 minutes for wider cakes. Bake the cakes for 10 to 14 minutes or until a cake tester inserted in the center comes out clean and the cakes are springy to the touch.

■ In a large bowl mix the shortening, sugar, Marshmallow Fluff, salt, vanilla, and jam together until light and fluffy. Scrape the bowl often to avoid lumps.

■ To assemble, spread one half of the cooled cakes with the filling, and the other half with 2 teaspoons of your favorite berry jam. You can also use fresh berries for extra flavor. Place halves together and press gently to spread filling to edges. Whoopie pies can be stored at room temperature for 2 or 3 days, but usually don't last that long.

Banana Whoopie Pies

Even in baking, best results come from using bananas at their peak of ripeness, not ones that are overripe. How to tell? Bananas are sweetest when they begin to show a sprinkle of freckles. Once the freckles become large enough to touch each other, the banana is past its prime. This recipe also hails from the folks at King Arthur Flour.

Yield: 8 to 12 whoopies

Cakes

½ cup (1 stick) unsalted butter, softened

½ cup brown sugar

¼ cup granulated sugar

½ teaspoon salt

1 teaspoon vanilla extract

1½ cups (3 medium to large) mashed bananas

2 large eggs

2 cups King Arthur Whole Wheat Flour, white wheat or traditional

1 teaspoon baking soda

1½ cups chocolate chips

¾ cup chopped walnuts (optional)

Filling

½ cup cream cheese, at room temperature

3 cups confectioners' sugar

1 teaspoon vanilla extract

1 to 2 tablespoons milk, as needed

¾ cup chopped walnuts (optional)

■ Preheat the oven to 350°F. Lightly grease two baking sheets, or line with parchment paper.

■ For the cakes: In a large bowl, cream together the butter, sugars, and salt until light and fluffy. Add the vanilla, and then the bananas.

■ The mixture will look curdled; that's okay. Beat in the eggs, one at a time.

■ Whisk together the flour and baking soda; add to the banana mixture, mixing until evenly combined. Scrape the bottom and sides of the bowl, then mix for 1 minute more.

■ Stir in the chips and walnuts.

■ Scoop the dough by the quarter cup for large cakes, and by the tablespoon for small cakes. Allow plenty of space between them.

■ Bake for 12 to 14 minutes, until the tops spring back when lightly touched with your finger, and the edges are a very light golden brown. Remove from the oven and cool on the baking sheet for 10 minutes before transferring the cookies to a rack to finish cooling completely before filling.

■ For the filling: Beat together the cream cheese, confectioners' sugar, and vanilla until smooth. Add just enough milk to make the mixture a spreadable consistency. Stir in the walnuts.

■ To assemble: Spread the bottom of one of the cakes with 2 tablespoons of the filling. Place another cakes on top of the filling, bottom side down.

KING ARTHUR FLOUR CO.

Nellie Moody Jones's Molasses Whoopie Pies

Moody's Diner on U.S. Route 1 in Waldoboro is one of those iconic Maine places—old-fashioned, but not pretentiously so. It's not retro, it just hasn't changed much since locals, truckers, and tourists started eating there in 1930. ¶ In 1999 Moody's whoopie pies were chosen one of the 100 top food finds by *Saveur* magazine. Since Moody's bakes many other items and cooks all the food for three meals a day from scratch, they don't sell whoopie pies wholesale and they rarely have time to bake any flavors but the traditional whoopie pie. Dave Beck, an owner and manager at the diner and grandson of Moody's founder, Alvah, says the following molasses whoopie pie recipe is rarely made at Moody's anymore, so if you want it—bake it! The recipe comes from *What's Cooking at Moody's Diner: 75 Years of Recipes and Reminiscences*, by Nancy Moody Genthner (Down East Books, 2003).

Yield: 8 to 12 whoopies

Cakes

1 cup sugar

1 cup vegetable shortening

1 teaspoon salt

2 eggs

1 cup molasses

1 teaspoon vinegar

4½ cups flour

1 teaspoon cinnamon

1 teaspoon ground ginger

2 teaspoons baking soda

1 cup hot, strong coffee

Filling

½ cup vegetable shortening

4 tablespoons Marshmallow Fluff

1 cup confectioners' sugar

milk, as needed to achieve spreadable consistency

NANCY GRIFFIN

A young molasses whoopie pie aficionado made this sketch, spotted at the 2009 Maine Whoopie Pie Festival

■ Preheat the oven to 350°F.

■ Combine and cream the sugar, shortening, and salt. Add the eggs, molasses, and vinegar, and mix thoroughly.

■ In separate bowl, sift together the flour, cinnamon, and ginger and stir into batter. Dissolve baking soda in hot coffee and add to remaining ingredients.

■ Drop by rounded teaspoonfuls onto a greased cookie sheet and bake 15 minutes. Cool and fill with marshmallow filling

■ To make the filling: Combine the shortening, Marshmallow Fluff, sugar, and milk and beat thoroughly, using just enough milk to make frosting spreadable.

Pennsylvania Dutch Pumpkin Whoopie Pies

After chocolate, pumpkin is the most popular whoopie flavor for the cakes, and the preferred filling usually contains cream cheese. This particular recipe, like so many of the best home-tested desserts, has passed from family to family and generation to generation. The woman who gave it to me got it from her daughter's college friend, who hailed from Pennsylvania Dutch country originally, so in my friend's household these warmly spiced treats were always known as Pennsylvania Dutch Whoopie Pies.

Yield: 18 to 20 whoopies

Cakes

4⅔ cups flour

1 tablespoon cream of tartar

2 teaspoons baking soda

1 teaspoon baking powder

¼ teaspoon salt

1 tablespoon plus 2 teaspoons ground cinnamon

1½ teaspoons ground ginger

1½ teaspoons ground allspice

1 cup butter, softened

1 cup flavorless vegetable oil

2⅓ cups brown sugar

1 cup fresh or canned pumpkin puree (the entire can works, too)

1 large egg

2 large egg yolks

1 tablespoon vanilla

¼ teaspoon freshly grated lemon zest

1⅓ cups quick-cooking oats

Filling

12 ounces cream cheese, softened

2 large egg whites

¼ teaspoon vanilla (or ½ to 1 teaspoon natural maple flavoring)

¼ teaspoon grated lemon zest

2¾ cups confectioners' sugar

■ Preheat the oven to 350°F and grease several baking sheets (or use parchment paper).

■ Thoroughly stir together the flour, cream of tartar, baking soda, baking powder, salt, cinnamon, ginger, and allspice in a large bowl.

■ In a second mixing bowl, beat the butter and oil at low speed until well mixed. Increase the speed to medium and continue beating until light and fluffy. Add brown sugar and beat until smooth. Beat in pumpkin, egg, egg yolks, vanilla, and lemon zest.

■ Gradually beat in the flour mixture (if mixer labors, stir in the last bit of flour by hand). With a wooden spoon, stir in the oats until incorporated.

■ Drop about 2½ tablespoons of batter at a time onto the baking sheets about 4 inches apart. Make them as round as possible using a blunt knife and swirling in a circular motion, and spread each batter mound out into an evenly shaped, 2¾" diameter round. Place in the upper ⅓ of the oven and bake for 10 to 12 minutes or until slightly darker at the edges. Remove from oven and let cool on sheets for 3 minutes. Using a spatula, transfer to a wire rack to cool.

■ To make the filling, cream together the cream cheese, egg whites, vanilla, zest, and ½ of the confectioners' sugar. Gradually add remaining sugar and beat until well blended and smooth. Refrigerate the mixture, uncovered, for at least 15 minutes, or cover and hold for up to 24 hours in the refrigerator.

■ To assemble, place 2 tablespoons of filling on the flat side of half the cakes. Let stand for a few minutes to allow the filling to set slightly. Top with remaining cakes, flat side down, trying to match like sizes so that the sandwiches are even. Let stand for 20 minutes to allow the filling to set a bit, otherwise the top may slide off.

TWO FAT CATS BAKERY

Whoopie Ways

U Ultimately, the whoopie pie is a sweet treat, unmatched in its deliciousness and decadence. Whether you're enjoying a lobster dinner in Maine or a pastoral jaunt in Pennsylvania, whoopies can be the perfect ending (beginning or middle) to many adventures. But there's more to the whoopie than its calorie count. The whoopie pie can transcend dessert altogether. So in this last chapter, we look at the ways of the whoopie.

Dessert Debauchery

Some people revel in the food-fight scene in the movie *Animal House* or delight in those contests where people catapult pumpkins great distances. Some of us think those kinds of hijinks are just a waste of good food.

But a contest in which people stuff as much of a particular food item down their gullets as possible is somehow acceptable. At least in the eating competitions food gets

NANCY GRIFFIN

into a human body, where it belongs, rather than splattering all over a wall or a field somewhere.

The Hershey Farm Restaurant and Inn launched its first Whoopie Pie Festival in 2004, calling it "The most delicious day in Lancaster County." The festival, at the Hershey Farm in Ronks, Pennsylvania, pulls in about 3,000 visitors, and untold thousands more have witnessed the championship whoopie pie–eating contest via video on YouTube.

The Pennsylvania festival puts a plate of ten traditional whoopie pies in front of each contestant. The group has three minutes to gulp down as many mini-sized, traditional cream-filled chocolate whoopie pies as they can. Contest officials give each contestant a new plate when they're close to finished with the first.

Ian Hickman, who styles himself "The Invader," swallowed thirty-six the first year, winning the contest handily. The second year, he beat his own record and downed an astounding sixty whoopie pies. The third year, he managed only forty-two, but, as all contestants agreed and photographs attest, the whoopie pies were bigger in 2008.

What does Ian "The Invader" Hickman do when he's finished gorging on dozens of whoopie pies? He joins his brother at the smorgasbord at the Hershey Farm Restaurant, naturally.

On Saturday, June 27, 2009, about 500 whoopie pie lovers crowded a parking lot in downtown

Dover-Foxcroft, a small factory town northwest of Bangor, for Maine's first Whoopie Pie Festival. Sponsored by the Center Theatre for the Performing Arts, a nonprofit organization that rescued, restored, and is running the old movie theater in town, the festival served a dual purpose: to raise funds for the theater and to raise awareness of the whoopie pie. Some public-spirited souls were also probably hoping the event would lure more visitors to town—and they couldn't have been disappointed.

Just as in Pennsylvania, the festival featured a whoopie pie–eating contest—two, in fact. Unlike the Pennsylvania event, the contest did not attract a voracious, competitive group of hungry adults with their eyes on the prize. Instead, in Dover-

WHOOPIE WISDOM

WHAT'S IN A NAME

True aficionados can follow in the footsteps of Caryn Elaine Johnson, who changed her name to Whoopi Goldberg when she decided to pursue a life in comedy. (As far as we know it had nothing to do with the dessert, though.

NANCY GRIFFIN

Foxcroft, youth prevailed—and different rules applied as well. Four youngsters entered the children's whoopie pie–eating contest, but instead of giving contestants a time limit for consuming as many whoopie pies as possible, the Maine event gave each contestant four whoopie pies and the first one to finish won. It was a rollicking and messy spectacle, and the crowd loved it.

When it came time for the adult contest, the two entrants turned out to be nearly as young as those in the children's event. A ten-year-old boy beat out his fifteen-year-old competition, who afterward admitted, "I didn't care if I won, I was just in it for the free whoopie pies!"

Whoopie Pie Activities

You can hunt for whoopies, run with them, play games with them, fling them about, and scream for them.

Instead of the tiny Easter egg, the Pennsylvania Whoopie Pie Festival

HERSHEY FARMS RESTAURANT AND INN

WHOOPIE
WISDOM

LOBSTAH
AND
WHOOPIES

Along with Maine lobster, Hancock Gourmet Lobster Company in Cundys Harbor, Maine, sells whoopie pies on its Web site, advertising them as "Part of the Food Pyramid in New England."

runs a whoopie pie treasure hunt where "kids of all ages" can scramble around in search of whoopie pies wrapped in brightly colored foil.

There's also a race in which participants grab a whoopie pie and run with it. Festival goers can play whoopie pie checkers (winners eat the captured pieces) or take part in a whoopie pie decorating contest. There are plans afoot to try to bake the world's biggest whoopie pie and make it into the *Guinness Book of World Records*.

The Keystone State event also features something called a Whoopie Pie Long Launch in which contestants throw whoopie pies at a target. Such a waste!

Another event is the Whoopie Yell Off, which officials describe as "a shout-out to all the delicious whoopie pies." Maine's festival had a similar competition—a Whoopie Pie Calling Contest. The contestants' attempts were loud and creative, but no whoopie pies answered the calls.

MAKE IT OFFICIAL

Amos E. Orcutt, president of the Maine Whoopie Pie Association, is behind the effort to have the whoopie pie declared Maine's official dessert.

"It started out a little tongue-in-cheek," explains Orcutt, but as people reacted to the idea with unbridled enthusiasm, he decided to pursue it. He's working to get the governor to declare Whoopie Pie Day, preferably in June, and as part of the declaration, also to designate the confection as the official Maine state dessert. "I envision a whoopie pie on every legislator's desk," says Orcutt. "Then, how could they refuse?"

A Whoopie Makeover

The whoopie pie craze has unleashed true creativity as bakers and consumers race to come up with ever more interesting constructions.

At the request of a bride-to-be, for instance, Kristen DuShane of Two Fat Cats Bakery in Portland, Maine, baked 140 whoopie pies, filled them with white frosting, decorated them with purple flowers and lavender ribbon to match the bride's color scheme, stacked them up to form a wedding cake, and topped them with a two-layer, seven-inch whoopie pie cake.

Jill DeWitt at Good Eats Boutique in Portland, Maine, erected a fully-decorated whoopie pie Christmas tree topped with a star-shaped cookie to adorn her shop for the holiday season. On another occasion she created a huge football-shaped whoopie pie cake at the request of a customer.

Regularly these days, home bakers are stacking whoopies up to create birthday cakes for kids, sticking flags in whoopie pies to celebrate Fourth of July, and dyeing the dough or filling for special holidays.

Food coloring can be tricky, so dyeing the batter may result in an unappetizing appearance. Better practice before the big day! If you're in a whoopie-making mood and can't find a holiday, make one up.

ISAMAX SNACKS BAKERY

There truly is no end to the versatility of the whoopie pie. So whether you bake them yourself, seek them out on the Internet, or pick them up fresh at the corner bakery, remember that there is a whole whoopie pie–loving nation that shares your affection for the wonderful whoopie's delectable, cakey, frosting-filled yumminess. Happy eating!